TABLE OF CONTENTS

61

WELCOME TO VIETNAM

As Lisa stepped off the plane in Hanoi, she was immediately captivated by the vibrant atmosphere and the mingling scents of street food wafting through the air. She embarked on a whirlwind adventure, immersing herself in the wonders of this enchanting country.

Her first stop was Halong Bay, where she embarked on a cruise through the iconic limestone karsts rising from the emerald waters. As the sun dipped below the horizon, casting a golden glow over the landscape, Lisa felt a sense of tranquility and awe.

Continuing her journey south, Lisa explored the ancient town of Hoi An, renowned for its lantern-lit streets and well-preserved architecture. Wandering through the narrow alleys, she marveled at the intricate details of the Japanese Covered Bridge and enjoyed the vibrant atmosphere of the bustling night market.

In central Vietnam, Lisa discovered the imperial city of Hue, where she delved into the country's royal past. Exploring the majestic citadel, she imagined the lives of the emperors who once roamed these grounds. She also indulged in the local cuisine, savoring the delicate flavors of Hue's renowned dishes.

Venturing further south, Lisa arrived in Ho Chi Minh City, a bustling metropolis where old and new seamlessly blend. She explored the historic landmarks such as the Reunification Palace and the War Remnants Museum, gaining insight into Vietnam's tumultuous history. Amidst the hustle and bustle of the city, she found solace in the serene beauty of the Saigon River.

From there, Lisa ventured into the Mekong Delta, a land of lush green rice fields and winding waterways. She boarded a traditional wooden boat and cruised along the tributaries, observing the local way of life and encountering the friendly faces of villagers.

As Lisa's journey came to an end, she reflected on the warmth and kindness she experienced from the Vietnamese people. Their genuine smiles and willingness to share their stories left a lasting impression on her.

Vietnam, with its stunning landscapes, rich history, and vibrant culture, offers an adventure of a lifetime. Whether it's exploring bustling cities, cruising through picturesque bays, or immersing oneself in the local traditions, Vietnam is a treasure trove waiting to be discovered.

Welcome to Vietnam, where every corner reveals a new story and every encounter leaves a lasting memory.

Embrace the spirit of adventure, and let the wonders of this extraordinary country unfold before you.

Embarking on a Journey of Discovery

Embarking on a journey of discovery in Vietnam is an experience that will ignite your senses and leave you with a deep appreciation for this enchanting country. From the bustling streets of Hanoi to the serene landscapes of the Mekong Delta, Vietnam offers a tapestry of culture, history, and natural beauty waiting to be explored.

As you set foot in Vietnam, you'll be greeted by the warm smiles of the locals, whose hospitality will make you feel instantly welcome. The vibrant streets of Hanoi will beckon you to immerse yourself in its rich history and charming old quarter. Take a cyclo ride through the bustling streets, visit ancient temples, and indulge in the tantalizing flavors of Vietnamese street food.

Journeying to the central region, you'll discover the ancient town of Hoi An, a UNESCO World Heritage site known for its well-preserved architecture and lantern-lined streets. Stroll along the riverfront, visit the iconic Japanese Covered Bridge, and lose yourself in the vibrant markets filled with handmade crafts and tailor shops.

No trip to Vietnam would be complete without exploring the stunning landscapes of Halong Bay. Embark on a cruise through the mystical limestone karsts that rise majestically from the emerald waters. Breathe in the fresh sea air, kayak through hidden caves, and witness a sunset that will take your breath away.

In the south, Ho Chi Minh City, formerly known as Saigon, awaits with its bustling markets, historical landmarks, and vibrant street life. Discover the Cu Chi Tunnels, a network of underground tunnels used during the Vietnam War, and delve into the city's rich colonial past at the Reunification Palace.

Venture into the Mekong Delta, a land of floating markets, verdant rice fields, and meandering waterways. Cruise along the river, visit local villages, and savor the flavors of fresh tropical fruits and delicious regional cuisine.

People and Culture

The people and culture of Vietnam are an integral part of the country's charm and allure. Vietnamese culture is a vibrant tapestry woven with a blend of indigenous traditions, Chinese influences, and French colonial legacies. The people of Vietnam, known as the Vietnamese, are warm, friendly, and deeply proud of their cultural heritage.

Hospitality is deeply ingrained in Vietnamese culture, and visitors will be greeted with genuine warmth and kindness wherever they go. The Vietnamese people are known for their humility, respect for elders, and strong family values. It is common to see multi-generational families living together and sharing a deep bond.

Vietnam is a diverse country with 54 different ethnic groups, each contributing their unique customs, traditions, and languages to the nation's cultural mosaic. The Kinh people, who make up the majority of the population, have a profound influence on Vietnamese culture.

Traditional Vietnamese customs and rituals are still practiced throughout the country. From the vibrant festivals celebrating the lunar calendar to the reverence for ancestors and the importance of spiritual beliefs, these customs showcase the deep-rooted cultural heritage of the Vietnamese people.

Vietnam's cuisine is renowned worldwide for its flavors, freshness, and diversity. Each region has its own culinary specialties, influenced by local ingredients and cooking techniques. Pho, banh mi, spring rolls, and fresh seafood are just a few examples of the delicious dishes that await food enthusiasts in Vietnam.

Art, music, and literature also hold a significant place in Vietnamese culture. Traditional Vietnamese music, such as the haunting melodies of the dan bau (monochord instrument) and the vibrant performances of the water puppetry, reflect the country's rich artistic traditions.

How to Use This Guide: Making the Most of Your Vietnam Adventure

This guide is designed to help you make the most of your Vietnam adventure by providing you with valuable information, insider tips, and recommendations. Here are a few key ways to use this guide effectively:

¶ Plan your itinerary: Start by reading through the detailed sections on different regions and cities in Vietnam. Take note of the attractions, activities, and points of interest that appeal to you the most. Use this information to create a personalized itinerary that suits your interests and time frame.

¶ Discover hidden gems: While popular tourist attractions are undoubtedly worth visiting, this guide also highlights hidden gems and off-the-beaten-path destinations. These hidden treasures will allow you to experience the authentic charm and beauty of Vietnam, away from the crowds.

¶ Get practical information: This guide provides practical information on transportation, accommodations, dining options, and more. Use this information to navigate your way through Vietnam with ease, ensuring a smooth and hassle-free journey.

¶ Embrace local culture: Vietnam is a country rich in culture and traditions. The guide provides insights into Vietnamese customs, etiquette, and local experiences. By understanding and respecting the local culture, you can engage with the people, try traditional activities, and truly immerse yourself in the vibrant Vietnamese way of life.

¶ Stay informed: Vietnam is a dynamic country with new developments and changes occurring regularly. Stay up to date with the latest information by checking for updates on travel advisories, local regulations, and safety guidelines. Additionally, make use of the recommended resources in the guide, such as websites and apps, to enhance your knowledge and stay informed throughout your journey.

CHAPTER 1: INTRODUCTION TO VIETNAM

Vietnam, located in Southeast Asia, is a captivating and diverse country known for its rich history, stunning natural landscapes, vibrant culture, and delicious cuisine. As an emerging travel destination, Vietnam offers a unique blend of traditional charm and modern developments, making it an exciting place to explore for travelers.

The country is bordered by China to the north, Laos to the northwest, Cambodia to the southwest, and the South China Sea to the east, providing a diverse range of landscapes. From the breathtaking limestone formations of Ha Long Bay to the terraced rice fields of Sapa and the bustling cities of Hanoi and Ho Chi Minh City, Vietnam has something for every traveler.

Vietnam has a complex history influenced by various dynasties, colonial powers, and the Vietnam War. This history is reflected in its ancient temples, historic sites, and war museums, offering visitors a chance to delve into the country's past and gain a deeper understanding of its resilience and cultural heritage.

The Vietnamese people are known for their warm hospitality and friendly nature. The country is home to a diverse mix of ethnic groups, each with their own traditions, languages, and customs. The bustling markets, vibrant street life, and colorful festivals showcase the lively and dynamic spirit of the Vietnamese people.

Vietnamese cuisine is renowned worldwide for its flavors, freshness, and variety. From the iconic pho noodles to the delectable banh mi sandwiches and aromatic street food stalls, food lovers will be delighted by the culinary delights that Vietnam has to offer. Whether you're sipping a traditional Vietnamese coffee or indulging in a seafood feast, the country's gastronomy will leave a lasting impression.

Traveling in Vietnam provides a unique opportunity to experience a blend of natural beauty, cultural heritage, and warm hospitality. Whether you're exploring the UNESCO World Heritage Sites, trekking through the mountainous regions, cruising along the Mekong Delta, or simply immersing yourself in the local culture, Vietnam promises an unforgettable journey.

This travel guide is your companion to uncover the hidden gems, immerse yourself in the rich heritage, and discover the natural splendors of Vietnam. It will provide you with essential information, insider tips, and recommended itineraries to ensure that you make the most of your time in this captivating country. Get ready to embark on an adventure of a lifetime in Vietnam.

Brief History of Vietnam

Vietnam has a long and complex history that spans over thousands of years. The earliest recorded civilization in Vietnam dates back to the Bronze Age, with the Dong Son culture flourishing in the northern part of the country. Throughout its history, Vietnam has been shaped by various kingdoms, dynasties, and foreign influences.

One of the most significant periods in Vietnam's history is the rule of the Chinese, which lasted for more than a thousand years. The Chinese occupation left a lasting impact on Vietnamese culture, language, and administration systems. However, the Vietnamese people managed to maintain their distinct identity and eventually gained independence.

In the 19th century, Vietnam faced colonization by the French, leading to a period of resistance and struggle for independence. This culminated in the August Revolution of 1945, when Ho Chi Minh declared the establishment of the Democratic Republic of Vietnam. The subsequent war with France, known as the First Indochina War, eventually led to the division of Vietnam into North and South.

The Vietnam War, which lasted from 1955 to 1975, was a significant event in the country's history. It was a conflict between the communist forces of North Vietnam, supported by the Soviet Union and China, and the anti-communist forces of South Vietnam, supported by the United States and its allies. The war resulted in significant loss of life and had a profound impact on the Vietnamese people.

After the war, Vietnam reunified as a socialist republic in 1976, with Hanoi as its capital. Since then, the country has undergone rapid economic development and reforms, embracing market-oriented policies while still maintaining its socialist political system.

Today, Vietnam is a thriving nation with a rich cultural heritage, bustling cities, and picturesque landscapes. Its history has shaped its identity and traditions, and visitors to Vietnam can explore ancient temples, historic sites, and remnants of the Vietnam War, gaining a deeper understanding of the country's past and its journey to the present day.

Vietnam Weather

Vietnam experiences a diverse range of climates due to its elongated shape and varying topography. Generally, Vietnam can be divided into three main regions: the north, the central, and the south, each with its own distinct weather patterns.

In the north, which includes cities like Hanoi and Halong Bay, there are four distinct seasons. The summers (June to August) are hot and humid, with occasional heavy rainfall. Winters (December to February) are relatively cool and dry, with temperatures dropping significantly in the northern mountainous areas. Spring (March to May) and autumn (September to November) offer pleasant temperatures and less rainfall, making them popular times to visit.

Moving to the central region, which includes cities like Hue and Hoi An, the climate is characterized by a tropical monsoon climate. The region experiences hot and dry weather from February to August, with temperatures peaking in July. The rainy season occurs from September to January, with occasional typhoons affecting the coastal areas.

In the southern region, which includes Ho Chi Minh City and the Mekong Delta, the climate is tropical, with high humidity year-round. The dry season lasts from November to April, with comfortable temperatures and lower humidity. The rainy season, from May to October, brings heavy downpours, but these are often short-lived and followed by sunny weather.

It's important to note that Vietnam's weather can vary within each region, and microclimates may exist in different areas. It's always a good idea to check the weather forecast before traveling and pack accordingly. Regardless of the season, Vietnam offers a range of experiences and attractions, so there's never a bad time to explore this beautiful country.

Best Time to Visit

The best time to visit Vietnam depends on the specific regions you plan to explore and the activities you want to engage in. Generally, Vietnam can be visited year-round, but different seasons offer varying experiences.

For the northern region, including Hanoi and Halong Bay, the best time to visit is during spring (March to May) and autumn (September to November). During these months, the weather is mild and pleasant, with less humidity and rainfall. The temperatures are comfortable for outdoor activities and exploring the stunning landscapes.

In the central region, which includes cities like Hue and Hoi An, the best time to visit is during the dry season, which runs from February to August. The weather is sunny and hot, ideal for beach trips and outdoor excursions. However, do keep in mind that central Vietnam is prone to typhoons during the rainy season, so it's best to avoid visiting during this period.

For the southern region, including Ho Chi Minh City and the Mekong Delta, the dry season from November to April is the best time to visit. The temperatures are pleasant, and the humidity is lower compared to the rest of the year. This period is perfect for exploring the bustling cities, enjoying river cruises, and visiting the floating markets.

Getting to Vietnam: Transportation Options and Airport Information

Vietnam is a popular tourist destination in Southeast Asia, and getting there is relatively easy thanks to its well-connected transportation infrastructure. Whether you're arriving by air or land, there are various transportation options available to suit your needs.

By Air:

Vietnam has several international airports, with the two main gateways being Noi Bai International Airport in Hanoi and Tan Son Nhat International Airport in Ho Chi Minh City. These airports are well-served by major airlines from around the world.

Noi Bai International Airport is located approximately 45 minutes from Hanoi city center. It offers a wide range of domestic and international flights, making it a convenient choice for travelers arriving in northern Vietnam.

Tan Son Nhat International Airport, located in Ho Chi Minh City, is the busiest airport in Vietnam and serves as the main gateway to the southern part of the country. It offers numerous domestic and international flights, connecting Vietnam to major cities worldwide.

By Land:

If you're traveling to Vietnam from a neighboring country, you have the option of entering by land. Vietnam shares land borders with China, Laos, and Cambodia, and there are border crossings available for travelers.

The main border crossings include:

- Vietnam-China Border: There are several border crossings between Vietnam and China, including the popular ones at Dong Dang (near Lang Son) and Lao Cai (near Sapa).

- Vietnam-Laos Border: The most common border crossing between Vietnam and Laos is the Friendship Pass located in Dien Bien Phu, which connects Vietnam's Dien Bien Province with Laos' Luang Prabang Province.

- Vietnam-Cambodia Border: The main border crossing between Vietnam and Cambodia is the Moc Bai-Bavet Border Crossing, which connects Ho Chi Minh City with Phnom Penh.

By Sea:

Vietnam also has several seaports that accommodate cruise ships and ferry services. If you're coming from nearby countries such as Thailand or Malaysia, you can consider taking a ferry to Vietnam. Popular ports of entry include Ha Long Bay, Da Nang, and Ho Chi Minh City.

Transportation within Vietnam:

Once you've arrived in Vietnam, there are various transportation options to help you navigate the country:

- Domestic Flights: If you're planning to visit multiple destinations within Vietnam, domestic flights are a convenient and time-saving option. Vietnam has several domestic airlines that offer regular flights to major cities and tourist destinations.

- Trains: Vietnam has an extensive railway network that connects major cities. Train travel is a popular choice for those looking for a scenic journey and a chance to experience the local culture.

- Buses: Buses are a common mode of transportation in Vietnam, offering both intercity and intracity services. They are a cost-effective option and provide access to destinations that may not have airports or train stations.

- Taxis and Ride-Hailing Services: Taxis are readily available in cities and larger towns. Ride-hailing services such as Grab are also popular and offer a convenient and reliable way to get around.

- Motorbikes: Renting a motorbike is a popular option for travelers who want to explore Vietnam independently. However, it's important to ensure you have the necessary licenses and insurance before riding a motorbike.

When planning your transportation in Vietnam, it's advisable to book flights in advance, especially during peak travel seasons. It's also a good idea to research local transportation options and plan your routes accordingly.

12 Reasons to Plan your Trip to Vietnam as your next Vacation Destination

If you're looking for your next vacation destination, Vietnam should be at the top of your list. This vibrant and diverse country offers a myriad of attractions and experiences that will leave you in awe. Here are 12 compelling reasons to plan your trip to Vietnam:

1. Natural Beauty: From the stunning limestone karsts of Ha Long Bay to the picturesque rice terraces of Sapa, Vietnam is home to some of the most breathtaking landscapes in Southeast Asia.

2. Rich Culture and History: Vietnam has a rich history dating back thousands of years, with influences from Chinese, French, and other Southeast Asian cultures. Explore ancient temples, historic sites, and learn about Vietnam's fascinating past.

3. Delicious Cuisine: Vietnamese cuisine is renowned worldwide for its fresh ingredients, bold flavors, and diverse dishes. Try the famous pho, banh mi, and fresh spring rolls for a mouthwatering culinary experience.

4. Warm Hospitality: Vietnamese people are known for their warm and welcoming nature. You'll be greeted with smiles and genuine hospitality wherever you go, making your trip even more memorable.

5. Vibrant Cities: From the bustling streets of Hanoi to the vibrant nightlife of Ho Chi Minh City, Vietnam's cities are vibrant and full of energy. Explore bustling markets, visit historical landmarks, and immerse yourself in the vibrant street food scene.

6. Beautiful Beaches: Vietnam boasts a coastline of over 3,000 kilometers, offering pristine sandy beaches and crystal-clear waters. Whether you're looking for relaxation or water sports, Vietnam's beaches have something for everyone.

7. Adventure Opportunities: With its diverse geography, Vietnam offers plenty of opportunities for adventure. Trek through lush

mountains, kayak in picturesque bays, or explore caves and waterfalls for an adrenaline rush.

8. Unique Festivals: Experience Vietnam's vibrant culture through its colorful festivals and celebrations. From the lantern festival in Hoi An to the Tet Lunar New Year celebrations, these events provide a unique insight into Vietnamese traditions.

9. Affordable Travel: Vietnam offers excellent value for money, making it an affordable destination for travelers. Accommodation, food, and transportation options are budget-friendly, allowing you to make the most of your trip.

10. Cultural Experiences: Immerse yourself in Vietnamese culture by participating in activities such as traditional cooking classes, lantern making, and visiting local villages to learn about the traditional way of life.

11. World Heritage Sites: Vietnam is home to several UNESCO World Heritage Sites, including the ancient town of Hoi An, the Imperial Citadel of Thang Long in Hanoi, and the Complex of Hué Monuments. Explore these historical and cultural treasures during your visit.

12. Breathtaking Landscapes: From the lush Mekong Delta to the terraced fields of the northern highlands, Vietnam's landscapes are diverse and awe-inspiring. Capture stunning photographs and create unforgettable memories.

CHAPTER 2: TIPS AND CONSIDERATION

When traveling to Vietnam, it's important to be well-prepared and informed to make the most of your trip. This section provides valuable tips and considerations to help you navigate Vietnam's unique cultural nuances, local customs, and practicalities. Whether you're a first-time visitor or a seasoned traveler, these tips will enhance your experience and ensure a smooth journey.

From understanding local customs and etiquette to managing your budget effectively, this guide will cover a range of essential tips. It will provide insights on how to stay safe, respect the local culture, and make informed decisions during your time in Vietnam. You'll also find practical advice on transportation options, communication, and important considerations for solo travelers, families, and LGBTQ+ travelers.

Additionally, we'll provide guidance on essential items to pack for your Vietnam trip, including suitable clothing for different regions and seasons. You'll learn about the local currency and money matters, as well as how to handle foreign transaction fees and avoid unnecessary expenses.

Furthermore, we'll explore the importance of travel insurance and provide recommendations for reliable insurance providers. We'll also discuss the benefits of using local SIM cards or portable Wi-Fi devices for convenient and affordable communication.

Visiting Vietnam on a Budget

Visiting Vietnam on a budget is not only feasible but also a fantastic way to experience the country's rich culture, stunning landscapes, and mouthwatering cuisine without breaking the bank. With a little planning and some savvy tips, you can make your trip to Vietnam affordable and enjoyable.

One of the biggest advantages of traveling in Vietnam is that it offers a wide range of budget-friendly accommodation options, from budget guesthouses to backpacker hostels and affordable hotels. Consider staying in local guesthouses or homestays for a more authentic experience and a chance to connect with locals.

Food in Vietnam is not only delicious but also incredibly affordable. Explore the bustling street food stalls and local markets to savor authentic Vietnamese cuisine at a fraction of the cost of dining in restaurants. Don't miss trying the famous pho, banh mi, and fresh spring rolls.

When it comes to transportation, Vietnam has a well-connected network of buses and trains that are economical options for getting around. Opt for local buses or sleeper trains to save money on transportation costs. You can also rent a motorbike to explore cities or rural areas, which offers both convenience and affordability.

Many of Vietnam's top attractions, such as natural wonders, historical sites, and cultural landmarks, can be explored on a budget or even for free. Research and prioritize the must-visit attractions and plan your itinerary accordingly.

To save on international transaction fees, it's recommended to carry a mix of cash (Vietnamese Dong) and use local ATMs when needed. Avoid currency exchange at airports and opt for reliable exchange centers in cities.

By being mindful of your spending, choosing affordable accommodation and transportation options, and exploring local cuisine and free attractions, you can enjoy an incredible trip to Vietnam on a budget. Embrace the spirit of adventure and immerse yourself in the beauty and charm of this captivating country without worrying about breaking the bank.

Navigating Vietnam: Public Transportation and Getting Around the Country

Navigating Vietnam and getting around the country is relatively easy and offers various transportation options to suit different preferences and budgets. Here are some key ways to get around Vietnam:

Domestic Flights: Vietnam has several domestic airports, making it convenient to travel between major cities like Hanoi, Ho Chi Minh City, Da Nang, and Hue. Domestic flights are a quick and efficient option, especially for long distances.

Trains: Vietnam's railway system connects major cities and offers a scenic way to travel across the country. Trains have different classes, including sleeper options for overnight journeys. It's advisable to book tickets in advance, especially during peak travel seasons.

Buses: Buses are a popular and affordable mode of transportation in Vietnam. They are available in different classes, ranging from local buses to deluxe sleeper buses for longer journeys. Bus routes cover most destinations, including rural areas and popular tourist spots.

Motorbikes: Renting a motorbike is a popular choice for travelers who want more flexibility and freedom. Motorbikes can be rented in major cities and tourist areas, but ensure you have a valid international driver's license and wear a helmet for safety.

Taxis and Ride-Hailing Services: Taxis are readily available in urban areas, and reputable companies like Vinasun and Mai Linh are recommended. Ride-hailing services like Grab are also widely used in Vietnam and provide a convenient and affordable way to get around.

Cyclos and Xe Om: Cyclos are three-wheeled bicycles with a passenger seat at the front, offering a unique way to explore cities like Hanoi and Ho Chi Minh City. Xe Om refers to motorbike taxis, where a driver takes you to your destination on the back of their motorbike.

Accommodation Options: Hotels, Resorts, and Homestays in Vietnam

Vietnam offers a wide range of accommodation options to suit different preferences and budgets. Whether you prefer luxury hotels, beachfront resorts, or immersive homestays, there is something for everyone. Here are some popular accommodation options in Vietnam:

Hotels: Vietnam has a wide selection of hotels, ranging from budget-friendly options to luxurious five-star establishments. Major cities like Hanoi, Ho Chi Minh City, and Da Nang offer a plethora of hotels with various amenities, including swimming pools, fitness centers, and on-site restaurants.

Resorts: Vietnam's coastal areas boast stunning resorts, particularly in popular destinations like Nha Trang, Da Nang, and Phu Quoc Island. These resorts often offer beautiful beachfront locations, spa facilities, multiple dining options, and recreational activities.

Homestays: For a more immersive experience, consider staying in a homestay. This option allows you to live with a local family, providing insight into Vietnamese culture and daily life. Homestays are available in rural areas, ethnic minority communities, and even in cities like Hoi An.

Boutique Hotels: Vietnam is known for its charming boutique hotels, which offer a unique and personalized experience. These smaller establishments often feature stylish decor, attentive service, and a cozy ambiance.

Hostels: Backpackers and budget travelers can find affordable hostels in popular tourist areas. Hostels typically offer dormitory-style accommodation with shared facilities, making them a great option for socializing with fellow travelers.

What to Pack For Your Trip

When packing for your trip to Vietnam, it's important to consider the diverse climate, cultural customs, and the activities you plan to engage in. Here are some essential items to pack:

° Clothing: Pack lightweight and breathable clothing suitable for Vietnam's tropical climate. Include comfortable walking shoes, sandals, a hat, and sunglasses. Carry a lightweight jacket or sweater for cooler evenings or when visiting mountainous regions.

° Weather-specific Gear: If you're traveling during the rainy season, pack a compact umbrella or a waterproof rain jacket. For beach destinations, don't forget to bring swimwear, a beach towel, and sunscreen.

° Modest Attire: Respect the local customs by packing modest clothing, particularly when visiting religious sites. Long pants, skirts, and shirts with sleeves are appropriate to cover your shoulders and knees.

° Travel Essentials: Include a reliable travel adapter for charging your electronic devices, a sturdy backpack or daypack for day trips, and a reusable water bottle to stay hydrated.

° Medications and Personal Care: Pack any prescription medications you may need, as well as a small first aid kit with essentials like band-aids, insect repellent, and hand sanitizer.

° Electronics: Bring a camera or smartphone to capture the beautiful sights of Vietnam. It's also advisable to have a power bank for charging your devices on the go.

° Travel Documents: Carry a photocopy of your passport, along with the original, and keep them in a secure place. Don't forget to bring your travel insurance details, flight tickets, and any other necessary travel documents.

Nightlife in Vietnam

Vietnam offers a vibrant and exciting nightlife scene that caters to a wide range of preferences. Whether you're looking for a lively clubbing experience, cozy bars, or cultural entertainment, Vietnam has something for everyone. Here's a glimpse into the nightlife in Vietnam:

Bustling Cities: Cities like Hanoi, Ho Chi Minh City, and Da Nang are known for their bustling nightlife. You'll find numerous bars, clubs, and lounges offering live music, DJ performances, and a variety of beverages to suit your taste.

Rooftop Bars: Vietnam's major cities boast stunning rooftop bars that offer breathtaking views of the skyline. Enjoy a cocktail while taking in the panoramic vistas of the city below.

Night Markets: Experience the vibrant atmosphere of Vietnam's night markets, such as the Hoi An Night Market or the Ben Thanh Night Market in Ho Chi Minh

City. Explore the stalls selling local street food, handicrafts, and souvenirs.

Cultural Shows: Immerse yourself in Vietnamese culture by attending traditional music performances or water puppet shows. These captivating displays showcase the country's rich heritage and artistic traditions.

Beach Parties: Vietnam's coastal areas, such as Nha Trang and Phu Quoc, offer beachfront bars and clubs that

 host lively parties. Dance the night away with the sand between your toes and the sound of crashing waves in the background.

Local Experiences: For a more authentic experience, visit local bars and cafes where you can mingle with the locals and enjoy the relaxed ambiance. Sip on Vietnamese coffee or try the famous Bia Hoi, a fresh and inexpensive local beer.

Shopping in Vietnam

Shopping in Vietnam is a delightful experience that allows visitors to explore the country's rich culture and vibrant markets. From bustling street markets to modern shopping malls, Vietnam offers a wide range of shopping opportunities for every taste and budget. Here's a glimpse into the shopping scene in Vietnam:

Street Markets: Vietnam is famous for its lively street markets, such as the Ben Thanh Market in Ho Chi Minh City and the Dong Xuan Market in Hanoi. These markets are a treasure trove of local handicrafts, textiles, clothing, and souvenirs. Bargaining is a common practice, so be prepared to haggle for the best prices.

Night Markets: Experience the excitement of Vietnam's night markets, where vendors set up stalls selling a variety of goods, street food, and local delicacies. The Hoi An Night Market and the Old Quarter Night Market in Hanoi are popular spots to explore in the evening.

Shopping Malls: Vietnam's major cities are home to modern shopping malls that cater to both local and international shoppers. These malls offer a wide range of products, including fashion, electronics, cosmetics, and household items. Some popular malls include Vincom Center and Saigon Centre in Ho Chi Minh City, and Vincom Mega Mall and AEON Mall in Hanoi.

Local Crafts: Vietnam is known for its traditional handicrafts, such as lacquerware, ceramics, silk, and woodwork. Explore specialty stores and boutiques to find unique pieces that showcase Vietnamese craftsmanship.

Tailor-Made Clothing: Vietnam is renowned for its skilled tailors who can create custom-made clothing at affordable prices. Hoi An is particularly famous for its tailor shops, where you can have suits, dresses, and other garments tailored to your specifications.

CHAPTER 3: TOP 10 MUST-TRY BEST CUISINE IN VIETNAM

Vietnam is a culinary paradise, offering a diverse range of flavors and dishes that will tantalize your taste buds. Here are the top 10 must-try cuisines in Vietnam:

1. Pho: Pho is Vietnam's most iconic dish, consisting of a flavorful broth, rice noodles, and various toppings such as beef or chicken, bean sprouts, herbs, and lime. It is a popular breakfast option and a comfort food enjoyed any time of the day.

2. Banh Mi: Banh Mi is a Vietnamese sandwich that fuses French and Vietnamese culinary influences. It typically includes a baguette filled with a variety of ingredients like grilled meats, pickled vegetables, cilantro, and chili sauce.

3. Bun Cha: Originating from Hanoi, Bun Cha is a dish featuring grilled pork served with rice

noodles, fresh herbs, and a tangy dipping sauce. It offers a perfect balance of flavors and textures.

4. Cao Lau: Cao Lau is a specialty of Hoi An, combining thick rice noodles, pork slices, bean sprouts, and fragrant herbs. The dish is known for its unique flavor, thanks to the water used from Hoi An's ancient wells.

5. Banh Xeo: Banh Xeo is a Vietnamese-style pancake made with rice flour, turmeric, and coconut milk. It is filled with shrimp, pork, bean sprouts, and herbs, and then wrapped in rice paper and dipped in a flavorful sauce.

6. Goi Cuon: Also known as fresh spring rolls, Goi Cuon is a healthy and refreshing dish. It consists of rice paper rolls filled with a combination of shrimp, pork, fresh herbs, and vegetables. It is often served with a peanut dipping sauce.

7. Bun Bo Hue: Originating from Hue, Bun Bo Hue is a spicy beef noodle soup that packs a flavorful punch. It features tender beef, rice noodles, lemongrass, and chili oil, creating a delicious and aromatic broth.

8. Cha Ca: Cha Ca is a famous dish from Hanoi, consisting of grilled fish marinated in turmeric, dill, and shrimp paste. It is served with rice noodles, herbs, peanuts, and a dipping sauce, creating a symphony of flavors.

9. Mi Quang: Hailing from Central Vietnam, Mi Quang is a noodle dish made with turmeric-infused rice noodles, pork, shrimp, and fresh vegetables. It is typically topped with crunchy rice crackers and a flavorful broth.

10. Ca Phe Trung: Vietnam's coffee culture is renowned, and Ca Phe Trung, or egg coffee, is a must-try beverage. It combines strong

Vietnamese coffee with a creamy egg yolk topping, creating a unique and indulgent flavor.

Money Matters and Saving Tips

When it comes to money matters in Vietnam, it's important to be prepared and make the most of your budget. Here are some money-saving tips and considerations:

Currency: The official currency of Vietnam is the Vietnamese Dong (VND). It's advisable to carry some cash in small denominations for convenience, especially in rural areas and local markets. However, major cities and tourist areas also accept credit cards.

Exchange Rates: Be aware of the current exchange rates and choose reputable exchange services or banks for currency exchange to ensure you get a fair rate. Avoid exchanging money at airports or unlicensed vendors who may offer unfavorable rates.

Bargaining: Bargaining is common in Vietnam, especially in markets and small shops. Don't be afraid to negotiate prices, but do so respectfully and with a smile. It's a great way to save money on souvenirs, clothing, and other items.

Budget Accommodation: Vietnam offers a range of accommodation options to suit different budgets. Consider staying in budget hotels, guesthouses, or hostels to save on accommodation costs. Research and book in advance to secure the best deals.

Street Food: Vietnamese street food is not only delicious but also affordable. Explore local food stalls and street markets to experience the authentic flavors of Vietnam without breaking the bank. Just ensure that the food is freshly prepared and hygienic.

Public Transportation: Utilize Vietnam's public transportation systems such as buses, trains, and local taxis to save money on transportation. They are often cheaper than private taxis and provide an opportunity to experience the local way of getting around.

Avoid Peak Seasons: Consider visiting Vietnam during off-peak seasons to save on travel expenses. Prices for flights, accommodations, and tourist attractions are typically lower during these times, and you'll also encounter fewer crowds.

Tap Water: It's generally recommended to drink bottled or filtered water in Vietnam to avoid any potential health issues. However, carrying a refillable water bottle and using water purification tablets or filters can help save money on constantly buying bottled water.

Tipping in Vietnam

Tipping in Vietnam is not as common as it is in some other countries, but it is still appreciated for exceptional service. While tipping is not obligatory, it is a gesture of appreciation for good service. Here's a story of how tipping was helpful to Lisa during her visit to Vietnam:

During her stay in Hanoi, Lisa went on a guided tour of the city. The tour guide, Mr. Nam, was knowledgeable, friendly, and went above and beyond to make the experience memorable. Lisa was impressed by his expertise and the personalized attention he provided.

At the end of the tour, Lisa decided to show her appreciation by giving Mr. Nam a generous tip. She handed him the envelope with the tip, expressing her gratitude for his excellent service. Mr. Nam was genuinely touched by her gesture and thanked her profusely.

A few days later, Lisa found herself in a tricky situation. She had forgotten her wallet at the hotel and needed some money for transportation back. She remembered Mr. Nam's kindness and decided to reach out to him for help. Not only did he remember her, but he also willingly lent her the money she needed without hesitation. Lisa was immensely grateful for his kindness and realized that her tip had helped build a connection beyond the tour itself.

Lisa's story that I just shared with you highlights the importance of tipping in Vietnam. While it may not be customary, it can go a long way in showing gratitude and building relationships with the locals. Tipping not only acknowledges excellent service but can also create a bond that may prove valuable in unforeseen circumstances. So, if you receive exceptional service during your visit to Vietnam, consider tipping as a way to express your appreciation and potentially receive assistance or goodwill in return.

Local Custom and Etiquette

When visiting Vietnam, it is important to be aware of the local customs and etiquette to ensure a respectful and positive experience. Here are some key aspects of Vietnamese customs and etiquette:

Greetings: The Vietnamese people value politeness and respect. When meeting someone, it is customary to greet them with a smile and a slight bow. Handshakes are also common, but wait for the other person to initiate it.

Respect for Elders: Vietnamese culture places great importance on respect for elders. Addressing older people with appropriate titles and showing deference is considered polite.

Removing Shoes: It is customary to remove your shoes when entering someone's home, temples, or pagodas. This shows respect for the cleanliness and sanctity of the space.

Dress Modestly: When visiting religious sites or rural areas, it is advisable to dress modestly and avoid revealing clothing. This shows respect for local customs and religious beliefs.

Dining Etiquette: When dining in Vietnam, wait for the host to invite you to sit and begin eating before starting your meal. Use chopsticks respectfully, and avoid pointing them at others. It is also polite to try a bit of everything served and compliment the food.

Public Behavior: Public displays of affection are generally not common in Vietnam. It is best to refrain from loud or boisterous behavior in public places as well.

Gift Giving: When invited to someone's home, it is customary to bring a small gift, such as fruit or flowers. Avoid giving gifts that are overly expensive, as it may cause the recipient to feel uncomfortable.

CHAPTER 4: HANOI (Capital City and Cultural Hub)

Hanoi, the capital city of Vietnam, is a vibrant and captivating destination that offers a unique blend of history, culture, and modernity. With its bustling streets, ancient temples, and French colonial architecture, Hanoi provides a fascinating glimpse into Vietnam's rich heritage.

As the cultural hub of the country, Hanoi is home to numerous historical landmarks and cultural attractions. The Old Quarter, with its narrow streets and traditional shop houses, is a maze of bustling markets, street food stalls, and ancient temples. The Ho Chi Minh Mausoleum, dedicated to Vietnam's revolutionary leader, and the nearby Hoan Kiem Lake, with its iconic red bridge and Turtle Tower, are must-visit landmarks.

Hanoi is also renowned for its vibrant culinary scene. Street food is a highlight, with an array of delectable dishes like pho (noodle soup), banh mi (Vietnamese sandwich), and bun cha (grilled pork with noodles) available in every corner. Don't miss the chance to savor these authentic flavors and immerse yourself in the local dining culture.

In addition to its cultural attractions, Hanoi offers a wealth of art galleries, museums, and theaters showcasing the country's contemporary art scene. The city comes alive at night with its bustling night markets, live music venues, and traditional water puppet shows, providing endless entertainment options for visitors.

Exploring Hanoi's bustling markets, enjoying a cyclo ride through the historic streets, and joining locals for a morning tai chi session in a city park are just a few ways to fully experience the charm of this vibrant capital.

Exploring the Old Quarter: History, Architecture, and Street Life

Exploring the Old Quarter of Hanoi is like stepping back in time to a bygone era. This historic neighborhood, also  known as "36 Streets," is a labyrinth of narrow alleyways and bustling streets that date back to the 13th century. With its rich history, charming architecture, and vibrant street life, the Old Quarter offers a fascinating glimpse into Hanoi's cultural heritage.

The Old Quarter is famous for its traditional shop houses, each specializing in a particular trade or craft. Walking through its streets, you'll find stores selling silk products, spices, jewelry, traditional crafts, and much more. The architecture of the buildings, with their narrow facades and unique rooflines, reflects a blend of Vietnamese, Chinese, and French influences.

As you wander through the Old Quarter, you'll encounter vibrant street life at every turn. Street vendors line the sidewalks, selling an array of local delicacies, from steaming bowls of pho to freshly brewed Vietnamese coffee. It's an opportunity to indulge your taste buds and experience the authentic flavors of Hanoi.

Don't miss the chance to explore the historic temples and pagodas that dot the Old Quarter. These ancient religious sites, such as Bach Ma Temple and Quan Thanh Temple, offer a peaceful respite from the bustling streets and provide insights into Vietnam's spiritual traditions.

In the evening, the Old Quarter comes alive with its bustling night markets and vibrant nightlife. The streets are illuminated with colorful lanterns, and you can immerse yourself in the lively atmosphere of outdoor cafes, bars, and live music venues.

Hoan Kiem Lake and Ngoc Son Temple: Tranquility in the Heart of Hanoi

Hoan Kiem Lake, located in the heart of Hanoi, is a serene oasis amidst the bustling city. Its name, which  means "Lake of the Returned Sword," is derived from a fascinating legend that adds to its allure. Surrounded by lush greenery and connected to the mainland by the iconic red-painted Huc Bridge, Hoan Kiem Lake is a tranquil retreat that offers a peaceful escape from the urban chaos.

At the center of the lake, you'll find Ngoc Son Temple, a picturesque pagoda sitting atop a small island. Accessible via the iconic red bridge, the temple is dedicated to Tran Hung Dao, a Vietnamese military hero, and features intricate architectural details and beautiful gardens. Inside the temple, you can explore its various halls, pavilions, and shrines, each with its own cultural and historical significance.

The combination of the lake's scenic beauty and the spiritual ambiance of Ngoc Son Temple creates a captivating atmosphere. Visitors can enjoy leisurely walks around the lake, taking in the peaceful surroundings, or sit by the water's edge and observe the locals engaging in activities such as tai chi, jogging, and socializing.

Hoan Kiem Lake and Ngoc Son Temple are not only significant cultural landmarks but also popular gathering places for locals and tourists alike. The area offers a respite from the city's hustle and bustle, providing a serene and scenic backdrop for relaxation and contemplation.

Temple of Literature: Preserving Vietnam's Scholarly Tradition

The Temple of Literature, known as Van Mieu in Vietnamese, is a revered historical and cultural site located in Hanoi, Vietnam. Built in 1070 during the Ly dynasty, it served as the country's first national university and remains a symbol of Vietnam's long-standing commitment to education and scholarship.

The temple complex is dedicated to Confucius, the revered Chinese philosopher, and also honors Vietnam's most accomplished scholars and intellectuals. Its well-preserved architecture reflects traditional Vietnamese design, with beautiful courtyards, pavilions, and ornate gates that showcase the country's rich cultural heritage.

Inside the Temple of Literature, you'll find tranquil gardens, picturesque ponds, and stone pathways that lead to various buildings and pavilions. One of the most significant structures is the Temple of Confucius, where statues and altars pay homage to the revered philosopher. The site also features steles mounted on stone turtles, which bear the names of exceptional scholars who passed the royal exams during the feudal period.

Visiting the Temple of Literature offers a glimpse into Vietnam's scholarly tradition and provides a serene escape from the bustling city. It is a place where locals and visitors alike can appreciate the importance of knowledge, learning, and the pursuit of wisdom. The tranquil ambiance and historical significance of the temple create a profound sense of reverence and inspire contemplation.

The Temple of Literature is not only a cultural landmark but also a popular destination for students seeking blessings for their academic endeavors. During exam seasons, it is common to see students and their families visiting the temple, praying for success and leaving offerings at the altars.

CHAPTER 5: HOI AN (Ancient Town and Cultural Delights)

Hoi An, located on the central coast of Vietnam, is a charming and historic town that captures the essence of Vietnamese culture and heritage. Known for its well-preserved ancient buildings, colorful lanterns, and vibrant atmosphere, Hoi An is a UNESCO World Heritage site that attracts travelers from all over the world.

Walking through the streets of Hoi An feels like stepping back in time. The town's architecture reflects a unique blend of Vietnamese, Chinese, and Japanese influences, showcasing its rich history as a major trading port in the 15th to 19th centuries. The narrow, winding lanes are lined with beautiful old houses, temples, and communal halls, creating a captivating ambience.

One of the highlights of Hoi An is the famous Japanese Covered Bridge, an iconic symbol of the town. This wooden bridge, adorned with intricate carvings and a small pagoda, spans the Thu Bon River and connects the Japanese and Chinese quarters. It is not only a significant historical landmark but also a popular spot for photographs.

Hoi An is also renowned for its traditional crafts and tailoring. The town is home to numerous tailors and artisans who can create custom-made clothing, shoes, and accessories. Visitors can explore the bustling markets and shops, and even participate in workshops to learn about traditional handicrafts such as lantern making, silk weaving, and pottery.

In the evening, Hoi An transforms into a magical wonderland as thousands of lanterns illuminate the streets and riverbanks. The Night Market offers a vibrant display of local goods, street food, and live performances, creating a lively and festive atmosphere.

Japanese Covered Bridge: Iconic Landmark of Hoi An

The Japanese Covered Bridge, an iconic landmark of Hoi An in Vietnam, is a symbol of the town's rich history and cultural heritage. This beautifully designed bridge is not only a functional passageway but also a testament to the harmonious blend of Vietnamese, Japanese, and Chinese architectural styles.

Built in the 16th century, the Japanese Covered Bridge  was constructed to connect the Japanese and Chinese communities in Hoi An. It was initially built as a way to reach the

Chinese quarter of the town, and later, a small temple was added to honor the deity responsible for the bridge's protection.

The bridge features intricate carvings and a distinctive arched roof, which is reminiscent of traditional Japanese pagodas. Its ornate decorations and elegant structure make it a truly mesmerizing sight. The bridge also serves as a symbolic representation of the historical and cultural ties between Vietnam and Japan.

Walking across the bridge offers a unique experience, as it provides breathtaking views of the Thu Bon River and the surrounding area. Visitors can admire the intricate details of the carvings, which include statues of dogs and monkeys at either end, representing the years in which the bridge was built and completed according to the lunar calendar.

The Japanese Covered Bridge is not only a historical landmark but also a popular spot for tourists to capture memorable photos. It serves as a gateway to Hoi An's

Old Town, with its narrow streets and ancient houses. The bridge is particularly enchanting during the lantern festival, when it is adorned with colorful lanterns, creating a magical atmosphere.

Ancient Houses: Preserving Traditional Vietnamese Architecture

The ancient houses of Hoi An, Vietnam, are a testament to the rich architectural heritage and cultural traditions of  the region. These well-preserved structures showcase the unique blend of Vietnamese, Chinese, and Japanese architectural styles, reflecting the historical influences that have shaped Hoi An over the centuries.

Walking through the narrow streets of Hoi An's Old Town, visitors will encounter a myriad of ancient houses, each with its own story to tell. These houses were typically built by wealthy merchants during the 17th and 18th centuries, and many have been passed down through generations, maintaining their original architectural features and traditional charm.

The ancient houses exhibit distinct characteristics such as wooden beams, ornate carvings, and tiled roofs. Intricate details and decorative elements can be found in the entrances, courtyards, and interior spaces. These houses often feature a combination of open-air courtyards, living quarters, and small altars for ancestor worship.

One of the remarkable aspects of the ancient houses is their ability to adapt to the local climate. With their well-designed ventilation systems, high ceilings, and strategic positioning, the houses offer a cool and comfortable living environment, even in the hot and humid weather of Hoi An.

Today, many of these ancient houses have been converted into museums, showcasing the history, culture, and daily life of Hoi An's inhabitants in the past. Visitors can explore the rooms filled with artifacts, furniture, and traditional artworks, gaining insight into the lifestyles of the people who once called these houses their homes.

Lantern Festival: Magical Illumination and Festive Atmosphere

The Lantern Festival in Hoi An, Vietnam, is a truly

 enchanting event that captivates locals and visitors alike. Held annually on the 14th day of the lunar month, this festival illuminates the ancient town with a kaleidoscope of colorful lanterns, creating a magical and festive atmosphere.

During the Lantern Festival, the streets of Hoi An's Old Town come alive with an array of lanterns, both big and small, adorning every corner. The lanterns are meticulously crafted from silk, showcasing intricate designs and vibrant colors. They are often shaped like lotus flowers, traditional Vietnamese symbols, or whimsical figures, adding to the charm of the town.

As dusk falls, the lanterns are lit, casting a warm glow over the streets and waterways. The reflection of the lanterns on the Thu Bon River creates a mesmerizing scene, as the water shimmers with the colorful lights.

The Lantern Festival is not just about the visual spectacle; it is also a time for cultural performances and traditional activities. Visitors can witness traditional music and dance performances, participate in lantern-making workshops, and enjoy delicious street food. The air is filled with laughter, music, and the scent of incense, creating a joyous and lively ambiance.

One of the highlights of the Lantern Festival is the floating lantern ceremony, where locals and tourists release paper lanterns onto the river, making wishes for good fortune and happiness. This breathtaking sight symbolizes the release of worries and troubles, as the lanterns float away, carrying hopes and dreams into the night sky.

CHAPTER 6: HO CHI MINH CITY
(Vibrant Metropolis and Historical
Significance)

Ho Chi Minh City, formerly known as Saigon, is a
vibrant metropolis and the largest city in Vietnam.
Steeped in history and bustling with energy, this city
offers a captivating blend of modernity and cultural
heritage.

As the economic and commercial hub of Vietnam, Ho
Chi Minh City is a bustling metropolis with towering
skyscrapers, bustling markets, and a vibrant nightlife. Its

streets are filled with a constant stream of motorbikes, honking horns, and the vibrant hustle and bustle of daily life.

One of the city's most iconic landmarks is the Reunification Palace, formerly known as the Independence Palace, which played a significant role in Vietnam's history. Visitors can explore its grand halls, presidential quarters, and underground bunkers, gaining insights into the country's struggle for independence.

For a glimpse into Vietnam's tragic past, the War Remnants Museum showcases the harsh realities of the Vietnam War through photographs, artifacts, and exhibits. It serves as a poignant reminder of the country's resilience and determination.

Ho Chi Minh City is also known for its vibrant street food culture, where visitors can indulge in a wide array of delicious and affordable dishes. From pho, the famous Vietnamese noodle soup, to banh mi, a delectable

Vietnamese sandwich, the city's street food scene is a true culinary delight.

A visit to Ho Chi Minh City is incomplete without exploring the historic district of Dong Khoi. Here, you'll find iconic landmarks such as the Notre-Dame Cathedral and the Central Post Office, which showcase the city's colonial past.

For those seeking a break from the urban chaos, the peaceful oasis of the Saigon River offers a relaxing escape. A leisurely boat cruise along the river provides stunning views of the city skyline and an opportunity to explore the nearby Cu Chi Tunnels, an intricate underground network used during the Vietnam War.

Cu Chi Tunnels: Underground Network of the Vietnam War

The Cu Chi Tunnels, located just outside of Ho Chi Minh City in Vietnam, are an extraordinary testament to the resilience and ingenuity of the Vietnamese people during the Vietnam War. This underground network played a crucial role in the war effort, serving as a base for the Viet Cong guerrilla fighters and a strategic stronghold against American forces.

Stretching over 250 kilometers in length, the Cu Chi Tunnels were an intricate maze of tunnels, bunkers,  trapdoors, and hidden chambers. They served as a vital lifeline for the Vietnamese soldiers, providing shelter, communication routes, and storage for weapons and supplies. The tunnels were ingeniously designed with multiple levels, ventilation systems, and booby traps to protect against enemy infiltration.

Visiting the Cu Chi Tunnels offers a unique opportunity to step back in time and gain insights into the harsh realities of the war. Guided tours allow visitors to explore a small section of the tunnels, experiencing firsthand the cramped conditions and the resourcefulness of the Vietnamese fighters. Crawling through the narrow passageways, visitors can imagine the hardships and sacrifices endured by those who lived and fought in the tunnels.

In addition to exploring the tunnels, visitors can also witness displays of war remnants, such as old weapons, booby traps, and hidden entrances. Educational exhibits provide historical context and further understanding of the war's impact on Vietnam.

War Remnants Museum: Documenting Vietnam's War History

The War Remnants Museum in Ho Chi Minh City, Vietnam, is a powerful testament to the country's  tumultuous history, particularly the Vietnam War. Formerly known as the

"Museum of American War Crimes," it showcases the devastating impact of the war through a collection of artifacts, photographs, and personal accounts.

Visiting the War Remnants Museum offers a sobering and thought-provoking experience. The museum's exhibits are divided into different sections, each focusing on a specific aspect of the war. From the consequences of Agent Orange to the brutality of war crimes, the museum provides a comprehensive portrayal of the conflict and its lasting effects on the Vietnamese people.

Photographs and documentary films vividly depict the harsh realities of war, capturing the human suffering, the courage of the Vietnamese people, and the atrocities committed during the conflict. Visitors can also explore outdoor displays showcasing military vehicles, aircraft, and artillery used during the war.

While the museum primarily focuses on the Vietnam War, it also highlights the country's struggles for independence and the resilience of its people. It serves as a reminder of the importance of peace, understanding, and the preservation of human dignity.

Ben Thanh Market: Shopping, Street Food, and Local Culture

Located in the heart of Ho Chi Minh City, Ben Thanh Market is a bustling and vibrant hub that encapsulates the essence of Vietnamese culture. As one of the oldest and most famous markets in the city, it offers a delightful sensory experience for visitors.

Ben Thanh Market is renowned for its extensive array of goods, ranging from clothing and accessories to  handicrafts, souvenirs, and local produce. Exploring the market's labyrinthine aisles, visitors can browse through a myriad of stalls, haggling for the best prices and immersing themselves in the vibrant atmosphere. Whether you're searching for traditional

Vietnamese garments, unique crafts, or delicious local snacks, the market has something to offer for every taste and budget.

Beyond shopping, Ben Thanh Market is a haven for food enthusiasts. Its food section is a culinary paradise, with a diverse selection of street food vendors and small eateries serving up mouthwatering Vietnamese dishes. From iconic dishes like pho and banh mi to regional specialties and refreshing tropical fruits, visitors can indulge in a gastronomic adventure and sample the rich flavors of Vietnamese cuisine.

Ben Thanh Market is not just a shopping destination; it's a cultural landmark that reflects the pulse of the city. It provides a glimpse into the daily lives of locals and offers an opportunity to engage with Vietnamese traditions and customs. Whether you're seeking unique souvenirs, trying authentic street food, or simply immersing yourself in the vibrant atmosphere, a visit to

Ben Thanh Market is an essential part of experiencing the lively spirit of Ho Chi Minh City.

CHAPTER 7: EVENTS, ATTRACTION AND ITINERARY

Vietnam is a country that captivates travelers with its rich history, vibrant culture, and stunning landscapes. From bustling cities to serene rural areas, there is an abundance of events, attractions, and itineraries that offer a diverse range of experiences for visitors.

The events in Vietnam showcase the country's cultural heritage and traditions. From traditional festivals like Tet (Lunar New Year) to vibrant street parades and lantern festivals, there are numerous opportunities to immerse yourself in the local culture and witness the colorful celebrations that define Vietnam.

The attractions in Vietnam are as varied as they are enchanting. From UNESCO World Heritage sites like Halong Bay, Hoi An Ancient Town, and Hue Imperial City to the natural wonders of Sapa and the Mekong Delta, there is no shortage of awe-inspiring sights to explore. Whether you're interested in history, nature, or adventure, Vietnam offers a wealth of attractions that cater to every interest.

Crafting an itinerary in Vietnam can be an exciting and fulfilling endeavor. With so much to see and do, it's important to plan your days carefully to make the most of your time. Whether you prefer to explore the vibrant streets of Hanoi, embark on a trekking adventure in the mountains, or relax on the pristine beaches of Phu Quoc, there are endless possibilities for creating a memorable itinerary that suits your preferences.

Whether you're a first-time visitor or a seasoned traveler, Vietnam offers an abundance of events, attractions, and itineraries that promise to make your journey unforgettable. From cultural festivals and historical landmarks to natural wonders and culinary delights, Vietnam has something to offer every traveler seeking a truly immersive and enriching experience.

Top 5 Events to Attend

Vietnam is a country known for its vibrant and lively events that showcase the rich cultural heritage and traditions of the Vietnamese people. Here are the top 5 events to attend in Vietnam:

1. Tet Festival: Tet, or the Lunar New Year, is the most important and widely celebrated festival in Vietnam. It marks the beginning of the lunar calendar and is a time for family reunions, feasting, and paying homage to ancestors. The streets come alive with colorful decorations, traditional music, and vibrant parades.

2. Hoi An Lantern Festival: Taking place on the 14th day of each lunar month in Hoi An Ancient Town, the Lantern Festival is a magical event that illuminates the streets with thousands of colorful lanterns. Visitors can enjoy traditional music performances, release lanterns into the river, and witness the town's enchanting beauty.

3. Hue Festival: Held every two years in the city of Hue, the Hue Festival is a grand celebration of Vietnam's cultural heritage. It showcases traditional music, dance, art, and culinary delights, offering visitors a glimpse into the rich history and royal legacy of the region.

4. Da Lat Flower Festival: Da Lat, known as the "City of Flowers," hosts a spectacular flower festival that attracts visitors from all over the world. The city's streets and parks are adorned with vibrant floral displays, and there are various activities such as flower parades, flower exhibitions, and cultural performances.

5. Nha Trang Sea Festival: Nha Trang, a coastal city in Vietnam, celebrates its vibrant marine heritage with the Nha Trang Sea Festival. The event features water sports competitions, traditional boat races, beach parties, and cultural

performances that highlight the local fishing communities and their connection to the sea.

Top 5 Attractions in Vietnam

Vietnam is a country brimming with captivating attractions that showcase its natural beauty, rich history, and cultural heritage. Here are the top 5 attractions in Vietnam that should not be missed:

Ha Long Bay: Located in the Gulf of Tonkin, Ha Long Bay is a UNESCO World Heritage Site and one of the most iconic natural wonders in Vietnam. The bay is famous for its towering limestone karsts, emerald waters, and picturesque islands, creating a breathtaking landscape that is best explored by boat.

Hoi An Ancient Town: Known for its well-preserved architecture, colorful lanterns, and vibrant atmosphere, Hoi An Ancient Town is a must-visit destination in Vietnam. Take a stroll through its narrow streets, admire the historic buildings, explore local markets, and indulge in delicious street food.

Cu Chi Tunnels: Located near Ho Chi Minh City, the Cu Chi Tunnels are an intricate network of underground tunnels that played a significant role during the Vietnam War. Visitors can crawl through the narrow tunnels, learn about the history and tactics employed by the Viet Cong, and gain insight into the resilience and ingenuity of the Vietnamese people.

Imperial Citadel of Thang Long: Situated in Hanoi, the Imperial Citadel of Thang Long is a UNESCO World Heritage Site that served as the political center of Vietnam for over a thousand years. Explore the ancient royal palaces, temples, and archaeological excavations that provide a glimpse into Vietnam's imperial past.

Mekong Delta: The Mekong Delta, often referred to as the "rice bowl" of Vietnam, is a vast and fertile region renowned for its lush green rice fields, winding waterways, and floating markets. Take a boat tour along the Mekong River, visit local villages, and experience the unique way of life of the people living in this region.

3 Days Vietnam Itinerary

If you have limited time but still want to experience the highlights of Vietnam, a 3-day itinerary can offer you a taste of the country's vibrant culture, natural beauty, and historical sites. Here's a suggested 3-day itinerary for Vietnam:

Day 1: Hanoi

Start your trip in Hanoi, the capital city of Vietnam. Spend the morning exploring the historic Old Quarter, where narrow streets are filled with bustling markets, shops, and traditional houses. Visit attractions such as the Temple of Literature and Hoan Kiem Lake. In the afternoon, take a cyclo ride around the city or visit the Ho Chi Minh Mausoleum and the One Pillar Pagoda. In the evening, immerse yourself in the vibrant street food scene of Hanoi by trying local delicacies at the night market.

Day 2: Ha Long Bay

Embark on a day trip to Ha Long Bay, a UNESCO World Heritage Site. Cruise through the emerald waters and marvel at the stunning limestone karsts jutting out of the sea. Explore hidden caves, go kayaking, and enjoy a delicious seafood lunch on board. Admire the breathtaking sunset over the bay before returning to Hanoi in the evening.

Day 3: Ho Chi Minh City

Catch a flight to Ho Chi Minh City, formerly known as Saigon. Begin your day with a visit to the historic Reunification Palace and the War Remnants Museum, which offer insights into Vietnam's turbulent past. Explore the bustling streets of District 1, including the Notre Dame Cathedral and the Central Post Office. In the afternoon, take a tour of the Cu Chi Tunnels, where you can learn about the underground network used by Vietnamese soldiers during the Vietnam War. End your day by exploring the vibrant Ben Thanh Market and indulging in local street food.

While a 3-day itinerary provides a glimpse into Vietnam's highlights, the country has so much more to offer. If possible, consider extending your trip to explore more regions such as Hoi An, Hue, or the Mekong Delta to fully immerse yourself in the beauty and diversity of Vietnam.

7 Days Vietnam Itinerary

If you have a week to explore Vietnam, you can create a fantastic itinerary that allows you to experience the country's diverse landscapes, rich history, and vibrant culture. Here's a suggested 7-day itinerary for Vietnam:

Day 1: Hanoi

Start your journey in Hanoi, the capital city of Vietnam. Explore the historic Old Quarter, visit the Temple of Literature and Hoan Kiem Lake, and immerse yourself in the local street food scene. Take a cyclo ride around the city to get a feel for its bustling atmosphere.

Day 2-3: Ha Long Bay

Embark on a two-day cruise in Ha Long Bay, one of Vietnam's most iconic destinations. Marvel at the limestone karsts, explore hidden caves, and enjoy activities like kayaking and swimming in the turquoise waters. Spend the night on a traditional junk boat, indulging in delicious seafood and taking in the breathtaking views.

Day 4: Hoi An

Fly to Hoi An, a charming ancient town known for its well-preserved architecture and lantern-lit streets. Spend the day exploring the UNESCO-listed Old Town, visiting historical sites, and trying local dishes. Don't miss the chance to get tailor-made clothing or take a boat ride along the Thu Bon River.

Day 5-6: Ho Chi Minh City and Mekong Delta

Fly to Ho Chi Minh City and embark on a city tour to discover its rich history. Visit the Reunification Palace, War Remnants Museum, and iconic landmarks like Notre Dame Cathedral and the Central Post Office. On day 6, take a day trip to the Mekong Delta, where you can cruise along the river, visit local villages, and experience the region's agricultural activities.

Day 7: Cu Chi Tunnels and Departure

Visit the Cu Chi Tunnels, an intricate network of tunnels used during the Vietnam War. Learn about the history and the resilience of the Vietnamese people. In the afternoon, shop for souvenirs at the bustling Ben Thanh Market before bidding farewell to Vietnam.

This 7-day itinerary provides a great mix of cultural exploration, natural beauty, and historical sites. Of course, there's much more to see in Vietnam, so if you have more time, consider extending your stay in each destination or exploring other regions like Hue or Sapa to delve deeper into the country's wonders.

5 Low-cost Hotel Options

Vietnam offers a range of affordable accommodation options for budget-conscious travelers. Here are five low-cost hotel options that provide comfort and value for money:

1. Backpacker Hostels: Perfect for solo travelers or those on a tight budget, backpacker hostels in Vietnam offer dormitory-style rooms at affordable rates. These hostels often have communal areas, shared kitchens, and organized social activities, providing a great opportunity to meet fellow travelers.

2. Guesthouses: Guesthouses are small, family-run establishments that offer basic but comfortable rooms at budget-friendly prices. They are often found in local neighborhoods and provide a more authentic experience. Guesthouses typically offer private rooms with shared facilities, making them an economical choice.

3. Budget Hotels: Vietnam has a wide selection of budget hotels that cater to travelers seeking affordable accommodation. These hotels offer clean and comfortable rooms with private facilities. While they may not have extensive amenities, they provide a comfortable stay at a reasonable price.

4. Homestays: For a more immersive cultural experience, consider staying in a homestay. Homestays allow you to live with a local family, offering insights into their daily life and traditions. Many homestays provide clean and comfortable rooms, home-cooked meals, and the chance to engage with the host family.

5. Boutique Hotels: While boutique hotels are often associated with luxury, Vietnam has a growing number of boutique hotels that offer stylish and comfortable rooms at affordable rates. These hotels provide unique and charming

accommodation options with personalized service, making them a great choice for travelers seeking a more intimate and boutique experience without breaking the bank.

5 Luxurious Places to Stay in Vietnam

Vietnam offers a range of luxurious accommodations for travelers seeking a pampering and indulgent experience. Here are five luxurious places to stay in Vietnam that provide top-notch facilities and impeccable service:

1. Luxury Resorts: Vietnam is home to numerous luxury resorts situated in breathtaking beachfront locations. These resorts offer spacious rooms or villas, private pools, stunning views, and world-class amenities such as spas, fine dining restaurants, and recreational facilities. They provide a perfect blend of relaxation and luxury.

2. Boutique Hotels: Vietnam boasts several boutique hotels that offer a unique and intimate experience. These boutique hotels often feature stylish and elegantly designed rooms, personalized service, and exclusive amenities. They are known for their attention to detail and creating a charming and memorable stay.

3. Heritage Hotels: Vietnam has a rich cultural heritage, and staying in a heritage hotel allows you to immerse yourself in the country's history. These hotels are often housed in restored historic buildings, offering a blend of traditional architecture and modern luxury. They provide a unique and culturally immersive experience.

4. Luxury Cruises: Explore Vietnam's stunning coastline and breathtaking landscapes aboard a luxury cruise. These cruises offer luxurious cabins, fine dining experiences, spa facilities, and various activities and excursions. Cruising along Halong Bay or the Mekong River is an

unforgettable experience of luxury and natural beauty.

5. Urban Luxury Hotels: Vietnam's major cities, such as Hanoi and Ho Chi Minh City, are home to luxury hotels that cater to discerning travelers. These hotels offer spacious and elegantly appointed rooms, upscale dining options, rooftop bars, and state-of-the-art facilities. They are located in prime locations, making it convenient to explore the city's attractions.

CHAPTER 8: UNDERSTANDING FOREIGN TRANSACTION FEES

When traveling to Vietnam, it's essential to understand foreign transaction fees to effectively manage your finances. Here are some key points to consider:

° *Currency Exchange:* When exchanging your currency to Vietnamese Dong (VND), be mindful of the exchange rates and any associated fees. It's advisable to compare rates at different banks or authorized money changers to get the best deal.

° *Credit Card Usage:* Credit cards are widely accepted in major establishments in Vietnam, but it's important to be aware of potential foreign transaction fees. Some credit card issuers charge a percentage of the transaction amount or a flat fee for international transactions. Check with your bank or credit card provider to understand their fee structure and consider using cards with lower or no foreign transaction fees.

° *ATM Withdrawals:* Using ATMs in Vietnam is a convenient way to access cash. However, be aware that both your home bank and the local bank may charge fees for ATM withdrawals. To minimize these fees, consider withdrawing larger amounts less frequently and using ATMs affiliated with major banks.

° *Dynamic Currency Conversion (DCC):* When making a purchase with your credit card, you may encounter DCC, where the merchant offers to convert the transaction amount into your home currency. While it may seem convenient, be cautious as DCC transactions often come with high fees and unfavorable exchange rates. Opting to pay in the local currency, VND, is usually the better choice.

° *Prepaid Travel Cards:* Consider using prepaid travel cards that allow you to load and spend money in VND. These cards often offer competitive exchange rates and may have lower fees compared to credit cards. Research different card options and compare their fees before making a decision.

Avoid Cell Phone Roaming Charges

When traveling to Vietnam, it's important to be mindful of cell phone roaming charges to avoid hefty fees. Let me share a story of Lisa's experience to highlight the importance of this matter.

Lisa was excited to explore the bustling streets of Ho Chi Minh City. As she landed at the airport, she received a notification from her mobile service provider about international roaming charges. Unaware of the potential costs, she continued using her phone as usual, browsing the internet, and making calls.

Days later, when she checked her mobile bill, she was shocked to see exorbitant roaming charges that significantly exceeded her budget. She realized that using her phone without a proper plan had resulted in unexpected expenses.

To prevent this from happening to you, it's crucial to take proactive measures. Here are a few tips to avoid cell phone roaming charges in Vietnam:

☐ Disable Data Roaming: Before departing for Vietnam, turn off data roaming on your phone to avoid unintentional data usage and charges. Use Wi-Fi networks available in hotels, cafes, and other public areas instead.

☐ Get a Local SIM Card: Consider purchasing a local SIM card upon arrival in Vietnam. This allows you to have a local phone number and access to affordable local data and call packages. Make sure your phone is unlocked to use a different SIM card.

☐ Use Messaging Apps: Instead of relying on traditional text messages, use messaging apps like WhatsApp, Viber, or Skype that work over an internet connection. This way, you can stay connected with your loved ones without incurring SMS charges.

☐ Wi-Fi Calling: Take advantage of Wi-Fi calling options available on some smartphones. If you have a stable internet connection, you can make calls through apps like FaceTime, Skype, or Google Voice without using cellular network services.

Consider an Vietnam SIM Card or Mifi Device

When traveling to Vietnam, considering a Vietnam SIM card or a portable Wi-Fi device, also known as a MiFi, can greatly enhance your connectivity and convenience during your trip. Here are some key points to consider:

Cost-effective Connectivity: Purchasing a Vietnam SIM card or renting a MiFi device can provide you with affordable and reliable internet access throughout your journey. You can enjoy data plans tailored to your usage needs, allowing you to stay connected without incurring high roaming charges.

Local Phone Number: Getting a Vietnam SIM card gives you a local phone number, making it easier for you to communicate with locals, make reservations, and navigate local services. This can be particularly beneficial if you plan to stay in Vietnam for an extended period or require frequent communication.

Flexibility and Convenience: Having your own SIM card or MiFi device allows you to stay connected at all times, regardless of your location. You can access maps, search for information, make online bookings, and share your experiences in real-time. This flexibility ensures a smoother travel experience.

Multiple Device Connectivity: With a MiFi device, you can connect multiple devices, such as smartphones, tablets, and laptops, simultaneously. This is particularly useful if you're traveling with a group or if you have multiple devices that require internet access.

Easy Availability: Vietnam SIM cards and MiFi devices are readily available at airports, local mobile shops, and online platforms. You can purchase or rent them upon arrival, making it a convenient option for travelers.

Download Offline Map

Downloading offline maps can be a smart and practical choice to navigate the country with ease. Here are some reasons why downloading offline maps for Vietnam is highly recommended:

Reliable Navigation: By downloading offline maps, you can access them even without an internet connection. This means you won't have to rely on cellular data or Wi-Fi networks to navigate through the streets of Vietnam. Offline maps provide you with reliable navigation, ensuring that you can find your way around even in remote areas or areas with limited connectivity.

Cost-saving: Using offline maps can save you money on data charges. Instead of constantly using your cellular data or purchasing a local SIM card, offline maps allow you to access maps and directions without consuming any data. This is particularly beneficial if you're on a limited data plan or trying to minimize your expenses while traveling.

Accurate Information: Offline maps are typically updated regularly, providing you with accurate information about streets, landmarks, and points of interest. You can trust the map data to guide you to your desired destinations and discover hidden gems in Vietnam without worrying about outdated or unreliable information.

Enhanced Exploration: With offline maps, you can plan your itinerary and explore Vietnam at your own pace. You can mark points of interest, create custom routes, and easily find nearby attractions, restaurants, and hotels. This allows you to make the most of your time in

Vietnam and discover places that may not be on traditional tourist maps.

Convenience: Offline maps are easy to use and can be accessed directly from your smartphone or tablet. Many map applications allow you to save specific regions or entire maps for offline use, ensuring that you have access to them whenever you need them.

Vietnamese Phrases and Language Tips: Basic Communication for Travelers

Vietnamese is the official language of Vietnam, and while English is spoken in tourist areas, knowing a few basic phrases can go a long way in enhancing your travel experience and connecting with the locals. Here are some essential Vietnamese phrases and language tips for travelers:

Greetings and Polite Expressions:
- Xin chào (Sin chow): Hello

- Cảm ơn (Gahm uhn): Thank you
- Xin lỗi (Sin loy): Excuse me/sorry
- Tạm biệt (Tahm byet): Goodbye
- Basic Conversation:
- Tên là gì? (Ten lah yee?): What is your name?
- Tôi tên là... (Toy ten lah...): My name is...
- Bạn có nói tiếng Anh không? (Ban koh noi tieng Anh khong?): Do you speak English?
- Tôi không hiểu (Toy koh hee-oo): I don't understand.

Ordering Food and Drinks:

- Một (Mot): One
- Hai (Hai): Two
- Xin một cái... (Sin mot kai...): One [item], please.
- Tôi muốn... (Toy muh-uhn...): I would like...
- Có thể được hóa đơn, xin? (Koh tay duoc hwa don, sin?): Can I have the bill, please?

Asking for Directions:

- Xin lỗi, tôi muốn đi đến... (Sin loy, toy muh-uhn dee den...): Excuse me, I want to go to...

113

- Bưu điện (Boo dee-uhn): Post office
- Nhà vệ sinh (Nha vay sin): Restroom
- Bến xe (Ben se): Bus station

Emergencies:

- Cứu tôi (Kyu toy): Help me
- Bác sĩ (Bahk see): Doctor
- Cảnh sát (Gahng saht): Police
- Tôi bị mất (Toy bee maht): I lost...

Language Tips:

Pronunciation: Vietnamese is a tonal language, meaning that the tone used to pronounce a word can change its meaning. Pay attention to the tone marks and practice pronouncing words with the correct tone.

Politeness: Vietnamese culture places importance on politeness. Adding "xin" (please) and "cảm ơn" (thank you) to your sentences shows respect and courtesy.

Non-verbal Communication: Vietnamese people often use hand gestures and facial expressions to communicate. Pay attention to these non-verbal cues to better understand the context of a conversation.

Learning Key Phrases: Besides the basic phrases mentioned, it can be helpful to learn additional phrases like asking for directions, negotiating prices, and expressing preferences in Vietnamese.

Example Conversation:

- Traveler: Xin chào. Tôi tên là Lisa. (Hello. My name is Lisa.)
- Local: Chào Lisa. Bạn có nói tiếng Việt không? (Hello Lisa. Do you speak Vietnamese?)
- Traveler: Xin lỗi, tôi không hiểu tiếng Việt. Bạn có nói tiếng Anh không? (Sorry, I don't understand Vietnamese. Do you speak English?)
- Local: Có, tôi nói tiếng Anh. Bạn cần giúp đỡ gì? (Yes, I speak English. You need help?)

CHAPTER 9: EXPLORING VIETNAM

Exploring Vietnam offers a unique and unforgettable experience for travelers seeking adventure, relaxation, and cultural immersion. From bustling cities to serene countryside, Vietnam has something to offer every type of traveler.

The country boasts a diverse range of attractions, including UNESCO World Heritage Sites, ancient temples, bustling markets, pristine beaches, and breathtaking mountain ranges. Whether you're exploring the narrow streets of Hanoi's Old Quarter, cruising through the picturesque limestone islands of Halong Bay, or wandering through the ancient ruins of Hoi An, you'll be captivated by Vietnam's beauty and charm.

Vietnam's history is also deeply ingrained in its culture, and visitors have the opportunity to learn about its past through museums, war remnants, and historic sites like the Cu Chi Tunnels and Imperial Citadel of Hue. Additionally, the warm and welcoming locals, with their traditional customs and rituals, add a special touch to your journey.

The country's cuisine is renowned worldwide, with its fresh ingredients, aromatic flavors, and diverse regional dishes. From pho (noodle soup) to banh mi (Vietnamese sandwich), and from spring rolls to local street food, Vietnam's culinary scene is a food lover's paradise.

National Parks and Preserves

Vietnam is blessed with an abundance of natural beauty, and its national parks and preserves offer a glimpse into the country's pristine landscapes and diverse ecosystems. These protected areas provide a sanctuary for wildlife, preserve natural habitats, and offer visitors the opportunity to explore Vietnam's incredible biodiversity.

One of the most famous national parks in Vietnam is Phong Nha-Ke Bang National Park, a UNESCO World Heritage Site. Located in central Vietnam, it is home to some of the world's largest cave systems, including the mesmerizing Son Doong Cave. Visitors can explore the park's lush forests, limestone mountains, and underground wonders, making it a paradise for adventure enthusiasts.

Another remarkable national park is Cat Tien National Park, situated in the southern part of the country. This tropical rainforest is a haven for wildlife, housing rare species such as the Javan rhinoceros, Asian elephant, and

Indochinese tiger. Nature lovers can embark on hiking trails, spot a variety of bird species, and take part in wildlife conservation efforts.

In the northern region, Ba Be National Park offers breathtaking scenery with its emerald lakes, limestone cliffs, and dense forests. The park is home to diverse flora and fauna, and visitors can enjoy activities like boating, trekking, and interacting with local ethnic communities.

Vietnam also has several marine protected areas, such as Con Dao National Park and Phu Quoc National Park, which encompass pristine coral reefs, vibrant marine life, and stunning beaches. Snorkeling, diving, and island hopping are popular activities for visitors to these coastal preserves.

Outdoor Activities

Vietnam is a haven for outdoor enthusiasts, offering a wide range of thrilling activities amidst its breathtaking landscapes. From towering mountains to pristine coastlines, there is something for everyone to enjoy in the great outdoors of Vietnam.

Trekking and hiking are popular activities, especially in the northern region where the majestic peaks of Sapa and Ha Giang beckon adventurous souls. The scenic trails take you through terraced rice fields, remote ethnic villages, and stunning valleys, providing a unique cultural and natural experience.

For those seeking adrenaline-pumping adventures, rock climbing and canyoning are available in places like Cat Ba Island and Da Lat. Scale limestone cliffs, abseil down waterfalls, and dive into crystal-clear pools for an exhilarating experience.

Water-based activities abound in Vietnam's coastal areas, with options like kayaking, snorkeling, and scuba diving. Explore the stunning limestone karsts of Halong Bay, or dive into the vibrant coral reefs of Nha Trang and Phu Quoc Island.

If you prefer a more leisurely outdoor experience, consider a cycling tour through the charming countryside of Hoi An or the Mekong Delta. Pedal along rural paths, encounter friendly locals, and witness the idyllic scenery that Vietnam is known for.

For nature lovers, bird watching and wildlife spotting are popular activities in national parks such as Cuc Phuong and Cat Tien. Get up close to unique bird species and spot elusive wildlife, including primates, deer, and reptiles.

Vietnam's diverse landscapes also offer opportunities for water sports like surfing, windsurfing, and kiteboarding in coastal areas like Mui Ne and Da Nang.

Whatever your preference, Vietnam's outdoor activities cater to all levels of adventure and provide unforgettable experiences in the midst of its natural wonders. So, gear up, embrace the beauty of Vietnam, and let the great outdoors become your playground.

Nature Tour

Embarking on a nature tour in Vietnam is a remarkable way to connect with the country's stunning natural landscapes and biodiversity. Vietnam boasts a wealth of natural wonders, from lush national parks to pristine beaches and awe-inspiring mountain ranges.

One of the highlights of a nature tour in Vietnam is exploring the dense jungles and diverse ecosystems of national parks like Cat Tien, Phong Nha-Ke Bang, and Ba Be. These protected areas are home to an array of wildlife species, including rare primates, exotic birds, and elusive reptiles. Trekking through the verdant forests, you can witness the beauty of towering trees, cascading waterfalls, and hidden caves.

For coastal beauty, the stunning islands of Halong Bay and the Con Dao Archipelago offer breathtaking vistas of emerald waters, towering limestone karsts, and hidden lagoons. Cruising through the turquoise waters, you can soak in the serenity of these natural wonders and partake in activities like kayaking and swimming.

In the central region, the mesmerizing landscapes of the Truong Son Mountain Range and the Hai Van Pass provide excellent opportunities for hiking and exploration. The scenic routes offer panoramic views of lush valleys, cascading waterfalls, and terraced rice fields.

The Mekong Delta, known as the "rice bowl" of Vietnam, offers a unique nature experience. Drift along the winding waterways on a traditional sampan, surrounded by lush vegetation and floating markets. Witness the daily lives of locals and marvel at the vibrant colors and scents of tropical fruits and flowers.

Nature tours in Vietnam also allow you to engage in responsible tourism practices and contribute to conservation efforts. Many tour operators emphasize eco-friendly practices and support local communities, ensuring that your visit has a positive impact on both the environment and local livelihoods.

CHAPTER 10: WHAT TO DO BEFORE TRAVELING TO VIETNAM

Before traveling to Vietnam, there are several important things to do to ensure a smooth and enjoyable trip:

¶ Check visa requirements: Determine whether you need a visa to enter Vietnam and apply for it in advance if necessary.

¶ Vaccinations and health preparations: Consult your healthcare provider to receive any recommended vaccinations for Vietnam and obtain necessary medications for common travel illnesses.

¶ Research the weather: Vietnam has diverse climates, so research the weather conditions during your travel dates and pack accordingly.

¶ Plan your itinerary: Decide on the cities and attractions you want to visit in Vietnam and create a rough itinerary to make the most of your time.

¶ Currency exchange: Familiarize yourself with the local currency (Vietnamese Dong) and consider exchanging some currency before your trip or upon arrival.

¶ Travel insurance: Protect yourself against unforeseen circumstances by purchasing travel insurance that covers medical emergencies, trip cancellations, and lost belongings.

¶ Learn basic phrases: Familiarize yourself with a few basic Vietnamese phrases, such as greetings, thank you, and asking for directions. This can enhance your interactions with locals and show respect for their culture.

¶ Pack essentials: Pack appropriate clothing, including lightweight and breathable fabrics for the tropical climate, comfortable walking shoes, and any necessary electronics or adapters.

¶ Inform your bank and credit card company: Let your bank and credit card provider know that you'll be traveling to Vietnam to avoid any issues with card usage.

¶ Research local customs and etiquette: Learn about Vietnamese customs and cultural norms to show respect and avoid unintentional offense.

Entry Requirement

When planning your trip to Vietnam, it is important to familiarize yourself with the entry requirements to ensure a smooth and hassle-free entry into the country. Here are some key points to keep in mind:

Visa Requirements: Check if you need a visa to enter Vietnam. Depending on your nationality and the purpose of your visit, you may be required to obtain a visa in advance or be eligible for a visa exemption or visa on arrival.

Passport Validity: Ensure that your passport is valid for at least six months beyond your planned departure date from Vietnam. Having a few blank pages in your passport is also recommended for visa stamps.

Visa Application: If you need a visa, follow the appropriate procedures to apply for one. This may involve submitting an application at the Vietnamese embassy or consulate in your home country or using an authorized visa service.

COVID-19 Requirements: Due to the ongoing pandemic, additional health and safety measures may be in place. Stay updated on the latest travel advisories and check for any specific COVID-19 testing, quarantine, or vaccination requirements before your trip.

Immigration Procedures: Upon arrival in Vietnam, you will go through immigration and present your passport, visa (if required), and any supporting documents. Fill out the necessary entry forms and comply with customs regulations.

Proof of Onward Travel: It is advisable to have proof of onward or return travel, such as a confirmed flight ticket, to show that you have plans to leave Vietnam within the allowed period.

Travel Insurance: While not mandatory, having travel insurance is highly recommended to provide coverage for any unexpected medical emergencies, trip cancellations, or other unforeseen events during your stay in Vietnam.

Travel Insurance

When traveling to Vietnam, it is important to consider getting travel insurance. Travel insurance provides coverage and protection for various unforeseen circumstances that may arise during your trip. It can offer financial assistance in case of medical emergencies, trip cancellations or interruptions, lost or delayed baggage, and other travel-related issues.

Medical emergencies can happen at any time, and having travel insurance ensures that you have access to quality healthcare without worrying about the hefty medical expenses. It can cover hospitalization, doctor's fees, and even emergency medical evacuation if needed.

Another benefit of travel insurance is trip cancellation or interruption coverage. If unforeseen circumstances such as illness, injury, or a natural disaster disrupt your travel plans, travel insurance can reimburse you for the non-refundable expenses you have incurred, such as flights, accommodation, and tour bookings.

Lost or delayed baggage is another common issue faced by travelers. Travel insurance can provide coverage for the loss, theft, or damage of your luggage and its contents. This can help ease the inconvenience and provide compensation for necessary items you may need to purchase.

Additionally, travel insurance can offer 24/7 emergency assistance services, such as travel advice, translation services, and help in locating medical facilities or legal assistance if required.

Before purchasing travel insurance for Vietnam, it is important to carefully review the policy coverage, including the exclusions and limitations. Consider factors such as the length of your trip, the activities you plan to engage in, and any pre-existing medical conditions you may have.

Safety and Preparedness

When traveling to Vietnam, it's important to prioritize safety and be prepared for your journey. Here are some tips to ensure a safe and enjoyable experience:

° *Research and plan:* Before your trip, familiarize yourself with the local customs, laws, and potential risks in the areas you plan to visit. Research reputable accommodations, transportation options, and popular tourist destinations.

° *Stay updated on travel advisories:* Check for any travel advisories or warnings issued by your government or relevant authorities regarding safety concerns in specific regions of Vietnam. Stay informed about any potential risks or security issues.

° *Take necessary health precautions:* Visit a healthcare professional well in advance to ensure you are up to date on vaccinations and medications recommended for travel to Vietnam. Carry a basic first-aid kit with essential supplies and any prescribed medications you may need.

° *Practice caution with food and water:* While Vietnamese cuisine is delicious, be cautious about consuming street food or raw/undercooked items. Drink bottled or purified water and avoid ice cubes in drinks to prevent gastrointestinal issues.

° *Secure your belongings:* Be vigilant with your personal belongings and valuables, especially in crowded areas or tourist hotspots. Use a money belt or a secure bag to keep your passport, cash, and important documents safe.

° *Stay connected:* Have a reliable means of communication, such as a local SIM card or portable Wi-Fi device, to stay connected and reach out for assistance if needed.

° *Respect local customs and culture:* Familiarize yourself with Vietnamese customs and traditions to show respect to the local culture. Dress modestly when visiting religious sites and be mindful of local etiquette.

° *Stay aware of your surroundings:* Be mindful of your surroundings and exercise caution, especially in crowded places, public transportation, and at night. Avoid displaying signs of wealth or carrying large sums of cash.

Cash at the Airport is Expensive

When traveling to Vietnam, it is important to be aware that exchanging currency at the airport can be more expensive compared to other options. Airport currency exchange services often charge higher fees and offer less favorable exchange rates, which can result in receiving less Vietnamese Dong (VND) for your money.

To avoid these extra costs, it is recommended to exchange a small amount of currency for immediate expenses upon arrival at the airport. However, for larger transactions, it is better to wait and exchange money at local banks, reputable currency exchange offices, or withdraw cash from ATMs located throughout the country.

Banks and authorized currency exchange offices typically offer more competitive rates and lower transaction fees compared to the airport. It is advisable to compare exchange rates and fees before making any currency exchange to get the best value for your money.

Additionally, using internationally accepted debit or credit cards for payments is another convenient option. Many hotels, restaurants, and shops in major cities and tourist areas accept cards, although it is recommended to carry some cash for smaller establishments and more remote regions where card acceptance may be limited.

To ensure a smooth financial experience, inform your bank or credit card provider about your travel plans to Vietnam in advance. This will help prevent any unexpected issues with your cards being blocked due to suspicious transactions.

DOs and DON'Ts in Vietnam

By following these DOs and DON'Ts, you can show respect for Vietnamese culture, connect with locals, and have a more enjoyable and culturally immersive experience during your visit to Vietnam.

- Dress modestly: When visiting religious sites or rural areas, it is respectful to dress modestly, covering your shoulders and knees.
- Greet with a smile: Vietnamese people appreciate friendly gestures, so a smile goes a long way in creating a positive impression.
- Learn basic Vietnamese phrases: While many people in Vietnam speak English, learning a few basic phrases like greetings and thank you can help you connect with locals and show respect for their culture.
- Respect local customs and traditions: Vietnam has a rich cultural heritage, so be mindful of local customs and traditions. For example, remove your shoes before entering someone's home or a temple.
- Bargain at markets: Bargaining is common in Vietnamese markets, so don't be afraid to negotiate the price when shopping for souvenirs or other items. It's all part of the experience.

- Try street food: Vietnamese cuisine is famous for its delicious street food. Don't miss the opportunity to try local specialties like pho, banh mi, and fresh spring rolls from reputable food stalls or local eateries.

- Keep your belongings secure: Like any other destination, it's important to keep an eye on your belongings to prevent theft. Use a money belt or keep valuables in a secure bag.

DON'T:

- Display public affection: In Vietnam, public displays of affection are not commonly seen, especially in more conservative areas. It is best to show restraint in this regard.

- Disrespect Buddha statues or religious sites: Vietnam has many Buddhist temples and pagodas. Treat these places with respect by not touching or climbing on statues and following any guidelines or rules provided.

- Use your feet to point at people or objects: Pointing with your feet is considered impolite in Vietnamese culture. Instead, use your hand or words to indicate something.
- Disrespect local customs and traditions: Avoid criticizing or mocking local customs, traditions, or beliefs. Show respect and try to understand the cultural practices, even if they may seem different to your own.
- Waste food: Vietnamese people appreciate food and wasting it is seen as disrespectful. Order only what you can eat and finish your plate as much as possible.
- Drink tap water: Tap water in Vietnam is not safe for drinking. Stick to bottled water or boiled water and avoid ice cubes in drinks if you are unsure of the source.
- Touch someone's head: In Vietnamese culture, the head is considered sacred, so it is impolite to touch someone's head, even in a friendly manner.

CONCLUSION

We hope this Vietnam travel guide has provided you with valuable information and insights to make your trip to Vietnam memorable and enjoyable. From the bustling streets of Hanoi to the scenic landscapes of Halong Bay and the vibrant markets of Ho Chi Minh City, Vietnam offers a wealth of cultural experiences, natural beauty, and delicious cuisine.

As you embark on your Vietnam adventure, we encourage you to share your experience and thoughts on this guide by leaving a review on the Amazon store. Your feedback will not only help us improve the guide but also assist other travelers in making informed decisions and planning their own journeys to Vietnam.

When writing your review, we kindly request that you refrain from sharing any images or maps from the book to avoid spoiling the content for future readers. Instead, focus on the usefulness of the information, the clarity of the writing, and how the guide helped enhance your travel experience.

We greatly appreciate your support and contribution to helping fellow travelers discover this travel guide and navigate their way through Vietnam with ease. Your review will serve as a valuable resource for others seeking a comprehensive and reliable guide for their own Vietnam adventure.

Thank you for choosing this Vietnam travel guide, and we wish you an incredible journey filled with unforgettable moments and meaningful experiences in this captivating country.

FAQ

Q: What is the currency used in Vietnam?

A: The official currency of Vietnam is the Vietnamese Dong (VND). It is advisable to carry some local currency for small purchases and in remote areas, although major tourist destinations and establishments may accept credit cards.

Q: What is the best time to visit Vietnam?

A: The best time to visit Vietnam depends on the region you plan to explore. Generally, the months from November to April are considered the most favorable, as they offer pleasant weather conditions in most parts of the country. However, specific regions, such as the North or the Central Highlands, may have different weather patterns.

Q: Is it safe to drink tap water in Vietnam?

A: It is generally recommended to drink bottled or filtered water in Vietnam to avoid any potential health risks. Many hotels and restaurants provide complimentary bottled water, and it is widely available for purchase.

Q: What are the visa requirements for visiting Vietnam?

A: Visa requirements vary depending on your nationality. Some countries are eligible for visa exemptions or visa-on-arrival options, while others may require a pre-approved visa. It is advisable to check with the Vietnamese embassy or consulate in your home country for the most up-to-date visa information.

Q: Is it customary to tip in Vietnam?

A: Tipping is not a traditional practice in Vietnam, but it has become more common in tourist areas. It is appreciated but not expected. In restaurants, a 5-10% tip may be given for exceptional service. Tipping tour guides, drivers, and hotel staff is also a personal choice based on the level of service provided.

Q: What are some must-try Vietnamese dishes?

A: Vietnamese cuisine is renowned for its flavorful and diverse dishes. Some popular dishes to try include pho (noodle soup), banh mi (Vietnamese sandwich), bun cha (grilled pork with noodles), fresh spring rolls, and banh xeo (Vietnamese savory pancake).

Q: Are vaccinations required before traveling to Vietnam?

A: It is recommended to consult with a healthcare professional or travel clinic to inquire about necessary vaccinations for visiting Vietnam. Commonly recommended vaccinations include hepatitis A and B, typhoid, and tetanus-diphtheria.

Tips for Solo Travelers, Families and LGBTQ Travelers

Solo Travelers: Vietnam is a safe and welcoming destination for solo travelers. To ensure a smooth trip, it's advisable to inform someone about your travel plans, stay in well-populated areas, and use trusted transportation options. Joining group tours or connecting with fellow travelers can also enhance your experience and provide a sense of security.

Families: Vietnam is a family-friendly country with plenty of attractions and activities suitable for all ages.

When traveling with children, plan kid-friendly itineraries, consider accommodation with family facilities, and pack essential items such as sunscreen and insect repellent. It's also recommended to familiarize yourself with local customs and be mindful of cultural differences.

LGBTQ Travelers: While Vietnam is relatively progressive compared to its neighboring countries, it's important to note that LGBTQ rights are still developing. Major cities like Hanoi and Ho Chi Minh City have a more open and accepting attitude towards the LGBTQ community. However, it's advisable to exercise discretion and be aware that public displays of affection may not be widely accepted in more conservative areas. Research LGBTQ-friendly establishments and events in advance, and consider connecting with local LGBTQ communities for guidance and support.

Regardless of your travel style or identity, it's always beneficial to research local customs and cultural norms, respect the traditions of the places you visit, and practice general safety precautions. Embrace the diverse experiences Vietnam has to offer and be open to connecting with people from different backgrounds. Remember to be mindful of your surroundings and trust your instincts while exploring this beautiful country.

Additional Resources and Contact Information

Δ *Embassy or Consulate:* In case of any emergencies or assistance needed, it's important to have the contact information of your country's embassy or consulate in Vietnam. They can provide support, guidance, and assistance if required.

Δ *Tourism Information Centers:* Vietnam has tourism information centers in major cities and popular tourist destinations. These centers provide maps, brochures, and helpful information about local attractions, transportation, and accommodations. They can also assist with travel arrangements and provide recommendations.

Δ *Local Tour Operators:* Engaging with local tour operators can enhance your travel experience in Vietnam. They offer a variety of guided tours, activities, and packages tailored to your preferences. They have in-depth knowledge of the destinations and can provide valuable insights and assistance.

Δ *Online Travel Forums and Websites:* Online travel forums and websites are valuable resources for travelers to Vietnam. These platforms offer a wealth of information, including travel tips, recommendations, and reviews from fellow travelers. They can help you plan your itinerary, find the best accommodations, and discover hidden gems.

Δ *Local Emergency Numbers:* Familiarize yourself with the local emergency numbers in Vietnam. The universal emergency number is 112, which can be dialed for police, fire, or medical emergencies. Additionally, note down important local contacts such as hospitals, police stations, and taxi services for convenience and peace of mind.

It's always advisable to have a reliable internet connection while traveling in Vietnam. This allows you to access online resources, maps, and communication apps. Consider obtaining a local SIM card or using portable Wi-Fi devices to stay connected throughout your journey.

Maps and City Guides: Navigating Vietnam's Cities and Regions

When traveling in Vietnam, having access to reliable maps and city guides is essential for navigating the cities and exploring the diverse regions of the country. Here are some tips to help you make the most of these resources:

Offline Maps: Before your trip, download offline maps of the cities and regions you plan to visit. This ensures that you can access maps even without an internet connection. Apps like Google Maps and Maps.me offer offline map options that can be a lifesaver when exploring unfamiliar streets.

Tourist Information Centers: Visit local tourist information centers in each city to pick up free city maps and guides. These resources often provide valuable information on popular attractions, transportation options, and recommended itineraries. The staff at these centers can also answer any questions and provide further assistance.

Guidebooks: Consider purchasing a guidebook specific to Vietnam or the cities you plan to visit. Guidebooks offer detailed maps, historical information, and insider tips on the best places to visit, eat, and stay. They can be a valuable companion throughout your trip.

Online City Guides: Utilize online city guides and travel websites to gather information about Vietnam's cities and regions. These guides provide detailed descriptions of popular attractions, recommended itineraries, and tips from fellow travelers. They often include interactive maps that can be customized based on your interests and preferences.

Local Recommendations: Don't hesitate to ask locals or fellow travelers for recommendations on places to visit, eat, or explore. They can provide valuable insights and suggestions that may not be found in guidebooks or online resources. Engaging with locals also enhances cultural exchange and enriches your travel experience.

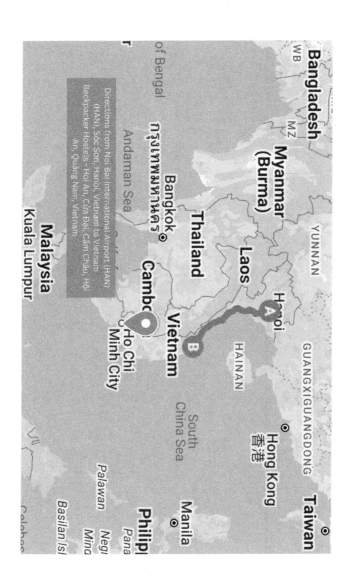

Directions from Noi Bai International Airport (HAN) (HAN), Sóc Sơn, Hanoi, Vietnam to Vietnam Backpacker Hostels - Hội An, Cửa Đại, Cẩm Châu, Hội An, Quảng Nam, Vietnam

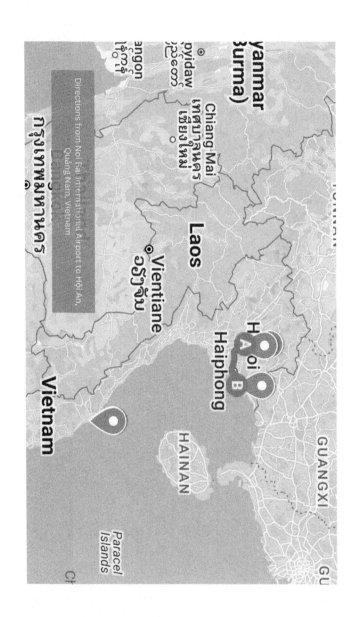

Directions from Noi Bai International Airport to Hội An, Quảng Nam, Vietnam

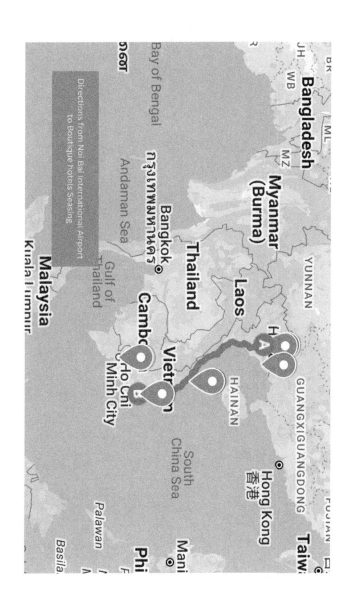

Directions from Noi Bai International Airport to Boutique hotels Seasing

153

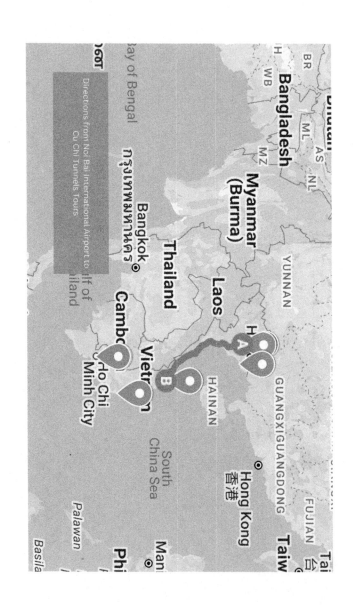

Directions from Noi Bai International Airport to
Cu Chi Tunnels Tours

154

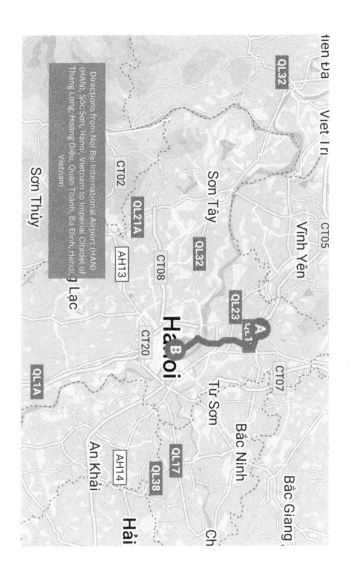

Directions from Noi Bai International Airport (HAN) (HAN), Sóc Sơn, Hanoi, Vietnam to Imperial Citadel of Thăng Long, Hoàng Diệu, Quán Thánh, Ba Đình, Hanoi, Vietnam

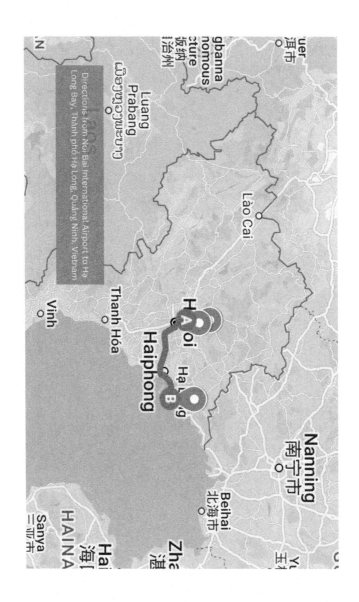

Directions from Noi Bai International Airport to Ha Long Bay, Thành phố Hạ Long, Quảng Ninh, Vietnam

156

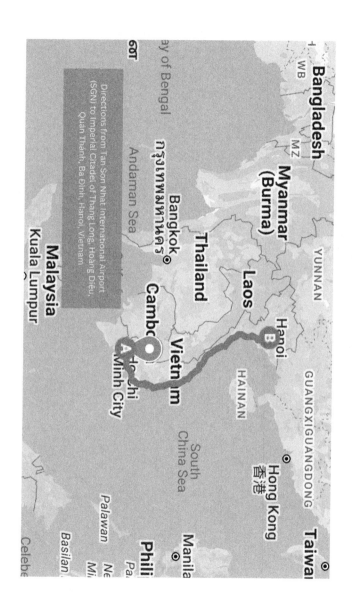

Directions from Tan Son Nhat International Airport (SGN) to Imperial Citadel of Thang Long, Hoàng Diệu, Quán Thánh, Ba Đình, Hanoi, Vietnam

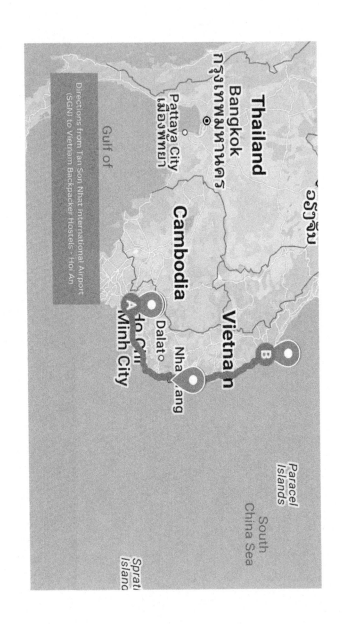

Directions from Tan Son Nhat International Airport (SGN) to Vietnam Backpacker Hostels - Hoi An

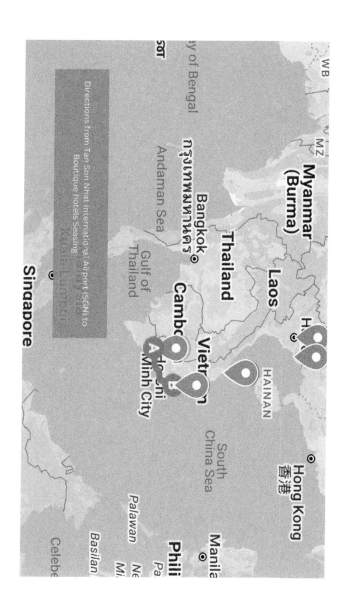

Printed in Great Britain
by Amazon

33804501R00089